Upcycle and Profit
Starting a Furniture Restoration and Resale Business

Table of Contents

Chapter 1. Introduction

Welcome to our Special Report, "Upcycle and Profit: Starting a Furniture Restoration and Resale Business" - a treasure trove of information brimming with inspiration and commercial savvy. If you have an eye for bringing back to life worn-out, vintage furniture pieces or if you're looking for a greener, more sustainable way to thrive in the retail industry, you've come to the right place. This report is a folksy, yet robust guide, that's been tailor-made for you. Inside, you'll find a world of practical, profit-laden advice right at your fingertips. Get ready to traverse through heartening success stories, valuable start-up advice, innovative restoration techniques, and exclusive marketing tips. Dissolve any doubts by buying this report, as we work together to add fresh life to old furniture, padding your wallet as you preserve, enrich, and redefine your love for one-of-a-kind, vintage beauty.

Chapter 2. The Charm of Upcycling: Understanding its Importance and Profitability

One can't help but smile at the way an old, forgotten piece of furniture suddenly springs back to life with just a little bit of tender, loving care. However, upcycling does more than just breathe new life into tired, old furniture. It is a sustainable, environmentally-friendly pastime that has transformed into a potentially profitable business venture. This chapter will delve into the charm and significance of upcycling in our society and discuss its potential for profitability.

2.1. The Philosophy Behind Upcycling

Upcycling is centered around the idea of taking something old or discarded and transforming it into something new and valuable. At its core, upcycling is a creative and innovative process that utilizes existing materials to improve upon the original item or transform it into something entirely new. Some might even describe it as a form of creative recycling.

Unlike recycling, which often involves breaking down materials to their core components, upcycling values the integrity of the original materials. Upcycling crafts rely on the quality and uniqueness of the materials, focusing on enhancement rather than destruction. Importantly, upcycling reduces the amount of waste that ends up in our landfills and lowers demand for new materials, thus playing a significant role in conserving our natural resources.

2.2. Upcycling and Environmental Sustainability

Our world is grappling with the problem of excessive waste generation. However, upcycling can play a role in mitigating this. Through creatively reusing and transforming everyday items and materials that would otherwise be destined for the landfill, upcyclers contribute to a more sustainable future.

Moreover, each piece of upcycled furniture contributes to reducing the carbon footprint associated with manufacturing new furniture. Producing new raw materials and then turning them into usable goods is an energy-intensive process. By upcycling old furniture into exciting, desirable pieces, we can repurpose valuable materials and reduce the demand for new goods.

2.3. Profitability Behind the Transformation

Now we delve into the matter of profitability. Like other businesses, starting an upcycling venture demands strategic planning, creativity, and consistency, but with relatively low startup costs. The initial financial requirement primarily depends on sourcing materials and tools, which, in most cases, can be found around the home or purchased second-hand.

The profitability of an upcycling business will largely depend on the uniqueness of your work and how well you're able to market it. People appreciate the exclusivity that comes with upcycled goods, along with the environmental sensitivity of these products. The quality of your handiwork coupled with strategic branding efforts makes for a potent mix that can be quite profitable.

2.4. Market Appreciation for Upcycled Furnishings

Consumer interest in upcycled products has surged over the years. This growing trend toward sustainable consumerism has increased the demand for upcycled items. Many people value the idea of transforming something old or discarded into something new and useful over the convenience of buying new items that might not last.

This uptake in consumer demand is good news for those considering delving into furniture upcycling for business. Research indicates that customers are increasingly willing to pay premium prices for sustainable, upcycled products, especially if they are unique and of high quality. Therefore, furniture upcycling can yield promising returns if done right.

2.5. Ingredients for Success

Given the rising demand for upcycled furniture, this venture harbors runaway potential. However, to tap into this potential, you would need to bring a few things to the table. An innate love for transforming frumpy to fantastic, an eye for potential in any given discarded piece, a knack for out-of-the-box thinking, and manual skills to refurbish and transform furniture are critical.

To augment your financial success, master the business side of things too — efficiently sourcing materials, setting appropriate price points, effective marketing, and branding, establishing profitable sales channels, and impeccable customer service.

In conclusion, upcycling isn't just a fancy buzzword. It's a viable, eco-friendly business venture that merges the beauty of crafting with the realities of accelerating consumer interests in sustainability. As this chapter explores, you can indeed make a successful living from upcycling furniture while contributing to a healthier planet. The upcycling journey stitches together stories..stories of transformation, reuse, and consideration for our environment. And it can be a profitable venture that marries passion with a paycheck.

Chapter 3. Amassing Your Tools: Essential Equipment for Furniture Restoration

The journey to making a profit from a furniture restoration and resale business begins with one critical step: assembling a comprehensive kit of essential tools. By catering to both novices looking to explore their creativity and commercial interest in the field and experts keen to diversify their toolkit for efficiency, this section aims to provide a thorough overview of indispensable equipment.

3.1. Basic Hand Tools

Any venture into furniture restoration inevitably begins with basic hand tools. Though they may seem too commonplace, they are the bread and butter tools.

- **Hammer**: Get a quality claw hammer – invaluable for dislodging nails.

- **Screwdrivers**: Have an array of sizes and types on hand, including flat-head and Phillips-head.

- **Pliers**: A few kinds – needle-nose, slip-joint and locking pliers, will help you tackle various tasks.

- **Chisels**: These will help in removing old glue or adhesives and are indispensable when working on joint repair.

- **Utility Knife**: For trimming, cutting veneer or scraping paint.

- **Tape Measure and Ruler**: Accuracy is key in restoration, and these tools ensure that.

3.2. Power Tools

While basic hand tools might serve for simple restoration, for a full-fledged business, you will need power tools to make work more efficient.

- **Power Drill**: For creating holes or driving in screws - a cordless drill offers flexibility.

- **Jigsaw**: Great for cutting into wooden furniture, particularly for intricate patterns.

- **Sander**: Sanding by hand can be a tedious task. Consider investing in both a belt sander for removing old paint or varnishes quickly, and an orbital sander for finer finishes.

- **Air Compressor with Spray Guns**: These provide an even layer of paint or finish and offer speed and better coverage.

Remember to always be mindful of safety when handling these tools. Invest in good quality goggles, gloves, and a dust mask.

3.3. Specialty Tools

Specialty tools are what distinguishes you from a novice restorer. This is not a comprehensive list, but includes tools that are often found to be useful in complex restorations.

- **Dowel Jig**: This tool helps align and drill precise holes for dowel joints.

- **Clamps**: Used to securely hold pieces together while glue dries - bar, C, and spring clamps each serve different purposes.

- **Router**: Allows for shaping, hollowing out, and decorative pattern cutting.

- **Veneer Saw**: Especially handy when dealing with veneered furniture.

3.4. Upholstery Equipment

Depending on your focus area within the restoration field, you might need upholstery tools to breathe new life into old seats.

- **Staple Remover**: A must-have to remove old coverings without damaging the frame.

- **Upholstery Hammer**: Useful for securing fabric tightly through tacks or nails.

- **Webbing Stretcher**: A tool used to easily fix and stretch the webbing or underlying support of upholstered chairs.

- **Upholstery Needle**: They come in curved, straight, and double-pointed variants for different upholstery applications.

3.5. Finishing Equipment

The finishing process is what adds the final polish to your restoration - the right tools can make a significant difference.

- **Brushes**: For applying varnishes, lacquers, paint, or wax.

- **Steel Wool or Scouring Pads**: Handy for buffing surfaces between each coat.

- **Rags**: For applying and buffing out wax.

- **Safety Equipment**: Important when handling chemicals - goggles, gloves, and a respirator.

3.6. Setting Up Your Workspace

The tools are just as good as the restoring environment. The spot should be large enough to work comfortably, well-lit, and well-ventilated (especially if you'll be painting or staining). Consider setting up a dedicated space for different tasks - disassembly and repair, sanding, painting or staining, and reassembly.

3.7. Looking After Your Tools

Keeping your tools in top form is essential for the best results. Regular cleaning and maintenance can extend their lifespan and ensure you work safely and efficiently.

Keep in mind - tools are an investment. Purchasing quality tools is a worthy investment for your business.

This comprehensive list should leave you well-equipped to start your journey into furniture restoration. Remember, tools can be accumulated gradually as jobs require, and as you become more familiar with the types of restorations you most enjoy working on. Set-up costs might seem high initially, but consider these as investments that will pay off exponentially as your business thrives. Whether you're just starting or are an experienced restorer, continually reviewing and updating your tool kit is vital to stay competitive and produce high-quality restorations.

Chapter 4. Mastering the Art: Basic and Advanced Furniture Restoration Techniques

While the thrill of discovery and the joy of profit might be central to your furniture restoration and resale venture, the heart of your business lies in the art of restoring furniture. Skilled restoration breathes new life into battered, overlooked pieces and transforms them into sought-after treasures. Whether you're just starting or seeking to refine your skills, this chapter will offer both basic and advanced furniture restoration techniques.

4.1. Learning Basic Wood Restoration Techniques

Basic wood restoration forms the foundation of any furniture restoration process. Establishing a solid grasp of these fundamental skills will help boost both the quality of your restorations and the efficiency of your operations.

To begin, you'll need to familiarize yourself with simple fixes for common wood furniture issues. Knowledge about filling chips and scratches, repairing minor loose joints, and fixing dents will equip you for routine restorations. Here are some easy steps to get you started:

1. Assess any damage: This first step involves thoroughly inspecting the furniture piece for any loose parts, scratches, stains or damage. This damage assessment broadly determines the kind of restoration needed.

2. Clean gently: It's crucial to clean the piece for removing old polish, wax, and dust. Mild soap and warm water can handle most jobs. Always pat dry to prevent excessive moisture from entering the wood.

3. Sand the piece: Start the sanding process with a 150-grit paper and progress to smoother grits. Fine-grit sandpaper will smooth the surface without overly disturbing the wood grain or causing unnecessary damage.

4. Stain or paint: Depending on the desired outcome, you may choose to stain the piece to enhance the natural wood grain, or paint it to achieve a more personalized look. Always apply consistent thin layers.

5. Apply finish: A finish, be it oil, wax, or varnish, seals the wood, enhances its appearance, and gives some degree of protection from elements.

4.2. Delving Deeper: Advanced Wood Restoration Techniques

As you progress and your skill set strengthens, you'll start to encounter furniture pieces requiring more extensive, specialized restorations. Advanced techniques come into play when dealing with intricate carvings, veneers, or specific types of wood, among other things.

One such method is French polishing, an intricate skill involving application of shellac using a rubbing pad to create a highly lustrous surface. Or you might find a piece featuring wood inlay, an exquisite detail where contrasting wood types or materials are embedded into each other to create decorative designs. Careful and delicate restoration is needed to preserve these details.

For furniture with missing or severely damaged veneer, a process is required to carefully remove old veneer and apply new one, working meticulously to match the existing veneer pattern. Wood bleaching is another specialized technique used to lighten darker spots on the furniture or to achieve a uniform lighter colour.

4.3. Repairing Upholstered Furniture

In addition to wood, you'll surely encounter upholstered furniture requiring a different set of restoration techniques, often centering around fabric renewal and structural repair. Successful upholstery restoration combines comfort, durability, and aesthetics.

Start with a careful inspection of the piece, addressing any structural issues before moving on to the fabric. If springs are loose, they might need to be retied or replaced. The padding might also need a refresh.

Once the structure is sound, turn your attention to the fabric. Whether you're replacing faded, worn-out fabric, or just giving a piece an updated look, choose high-quality, durable materials that match the style and period of the furniture. Brush up on your sewing skills, because stitching, buttoning, and edging will be essential to your upholstery work.

4.4. Adding the Final Touches

Successful restorations often hinge on the finishing touches that bring out the best in each piece. This can incorporate applying gilding to ornate carvings, installing hardware, or distressing reclaimed wood.

You can consider replacing hardware such as knobs, pulls, or hinges, keeping in mind that authenticity is essential. Pay attention to the little details that will make the finished piece stand out— small enhancements can dramatically increase the furniture's marketability and your profit potential.

Whether you are a novice or a seasoned restorer, continuous learning and practice remain invaluable. The most seasoned furniture restorers would tell you, every piece is a unique challenge with its specific demands. Keep the passion for restoration alive, learn from every mistake and success, and enjoy the journey as you turn old into gold.

Chapter 5. Spotting the Diamonds in the Rough: Tips for Sourcing Furniture

The pursuit of finding the perfect, upcycle-friendly vintage furniture is an art in and of itself. It requires a discerning eye, a knack for bargaining, and persistence. Embarking on your treasure hunt begins with knowing where to look, and then understanding what to look for.

5.1. Where to Source Your Furniture

One person's trash is indeed another's treasure when it comes to sourcing furniture. The key is to be creative and remain opportunistic about where you find your potential pieces.

1. **Garage Sales and Estate Sales:** These events are gold mines for furniture hunters. Families looking to declutter or dispose of their older furniture often put up pieces for sale at significantly lower prices than in a vintage shop. Be attentive to local listings and classifieds for such sales.

2. **Thrift Stores and Charity Shops:** These establishments frequently receive donations of used furniture. While this requires a bit of persistent rummaging, the payoff can be significant. Plus, your purchase goes towards supporting charitable causes.

3. **Flea Markets:** Here, sellers come from diverse backgrounds, contributing to a wide variety of pieces from different eras and styles. Flea markets are one of the best places to find unique and rare items.

4. **Online Marketplaces:** Websites like eBay, Craigslist, and even

Facebook Marketplace host a plethora of used furniture options, often at negotiable prices. Remember to factor in shipment costs when buying online.

5. **Auctions:** Physical or online auctions can introduce you to some fantastic finds. Be aware; prices can escalate quickly in a bidding war. It's essential to know your spending limit before participating.

5.2. What to Look for in Vintage Furniture

Once you know where to shop, understanding what to buy becomes crucial. A keen understanding of furniture's potential post-restoration can be the difference-maker in your venture.

1. **Resilient Materials:** Hardwoods like oak, teak, and mahogany tend to survive the test of time better than softwoods. If a piece is light yet strong, it often signifies good quality wood.

2. **Construction Quality:** Look for signs of good craftsmanship, such as tight-fitting joints and smoothly functioning drawers or doors. The presence of dovetail joints typically indicates high-quality construction.

3. **Restoration Potential:** Evaluate what it'll take to restore the piece. A worn-out finish can be relatively easy to fix, but broken elements may require expert skills or be too costly to make restoration profitable.

4. **Brand and Era:** If the furniture is identifiable with a particular brand or era, it may have added value. Certain styles like mid-century modern or brands like Ercol can fetch higher resale prices.

5. **Uniqueness:** One-of-a-kind items, such as a piece with intricate designs or rare features, often yield higher margins when restored and resold.

5.3. Haggling: The Art of Bargaining

Whether you're at a garage sale or an auction, mastering negotiation can help you keep costs low, increasing your eventual profit.

1. **Do Your Homework:** Research standard prices for various furniture types and styles. Knowing the average cost can provide you with a strong bargaining point.

2. **Inspect Thoroughly:** Make sure you inspect the piece for any damage that can further justify a lowered price.

3. **Don't Show Too Much Enthusiasm:** If a seller senses your interest, they may be less willing to negotiate. Keep a neutral demeanor while examining goods.

4. **Be Prepared to Walk Away:** Sometimes, you won't be able to negotiate a price that makes sense for you. Recognize when it's time to step back; there will always be other opportunities.

5.4. Developing a Sharp Eye: Knowledge and Practice

In the early stages, you may find it challenging to spot profitable pieces. Luckily, like any skill, this can be improved with practice and knowledge.

1. **Familiarize Yourself with Different Styles:** Learn about various periods and styles of furniture. Books, websites, museums, or even simply browsing antique shops can provide a solid base of knowledge.

2. **Practice Identifying Woods and Materials:** Knowing what different woods and materials look like, and how they wear over time, can give valuable insights into a piece's value and potential.

3. **Touch and Smell:** Older, quality wood furniture often has a

distinct smell—an intriguing mix of polish and age. Running your fingers over the piece can give you an insight into its condition.

In the final analysis, sourcing furniture for restoration and resale requires tact, market understanding, and a love for the process. As you delve deeper into this business, you will fine-tune your methods and instincts, both of which will prove invaluable in your quest for diamonds in the rough. The marriage of patience, knowledge, and a keen eye for detail can yield impressive results in the domain of furniture upcycling and reselling.

Chapter 6. Business Model Canvas: Building Your Restoration and Resale Plan

Starting a restoration and resale business involves many moving parts. You are not merely in the business of buying and selling furniture; you are in the industry of imbuing life into well-loved items, retelling their histories, and retouching their appearance with your unique perspective. This endeavor involves a careful understanding of markets, a fine craft, and an ability to curate experiences for customers.

Your business model is the backbone of your business; it serves as the blueprint that outlines your company's structure, from the value proposition to your revenue streams. Building a business model canvas is your first step towards a sustainable, creative, and profitable venture in restoration and resale.

6.1. Defining Your Value Proposition

Your value proposition is the unique value that your restoration and resale business offers to its customers. It's your magnetic appeal: it justifies why customers should purchase your goods, and what makes you stand out from other vintage furniture competitors.

In defining your value proposition, consider the following:

- What type of furniture do you want to focus on? Will it be shabby chic pieces, mid-century modern fixtures, or antique heirlooms?
- In what condition will you find these pieces, and how do you intend to restore and transform them?
- How do you add uniqueness to every piece?

- How do you ensure sustainability and quality in your restoration techniques?

6.2. Identifying Key Partnerships and Suppliers

Your key partnerships are the companies or individuals that can help you impact your business positively. These are your suppliers, business alliances, or even mentors in the restoration field. It's important to identify your partners early in the process to streamline the other aspects of your business.

Consider these when you identify your key partners:

- Pinpoint the types of furniture you need and where to source them.
- Form alliances or partnerships with other retail shops where you can resell your restored items.
- Foster good relationships with upholstery and reparation shops, as they can be vital for your restoration efforts.

6.3. Establishing Your Key Activities

Key activities are the actions you need to carry out to run your business successfully. These encompass sourcing pieces, restoring, pricing accurately, and retailing.

Consider:

- Creating a step-by-step guide of your restoration process. This can range from scouting for items, dismantling, repurposing to finishing touches.
- Develop a robust pricing strategy to capture your restoration effort, minimal overheads, and deserved profit.

- Identify ways on how to attract and retain customers.

6.4. Forming Your Customer Relationships

Building a customer-centric business is pivotal for any retail company. You are not just selling furniture; you are selling experiences, emotions tied to one-of-a-kinds, and memories that come with vintage furniture.

To form strong customer relationships:

- Understand your customer base. Determine who will be interested in your specific style and type of furniture.
- Leverage social media and other channels to foster interaction and generate leads.
- Address any inquiry or issue promptly and professionally.

6.5. Building Your Channels

Your channels refer to how your product reaches your customers. As a restoration and resale business, you have both physical and digital outlets.

To build effective channels:

- Look into options such as a physical store, online marketplace, or even antique fairs and markets.
- Offering delivery services can also be a beneficial addition.
- Ensure that your digital platforms reflect your brand's identity and the value of your pieces.

6.6. Defining Your Cost Structure and Revenue Streams

The cost structure includes direct costs, fixed and variable costs related to the business. Include restoration expenses, overheads, transportation, labor, and other costs.

For revenue streams, it's not only about selling the furniture:

- Think about potential partnerships, cross-selling, or up-selling techniques.
- You might also wish to expand into reupholstery services, or perhaps teach restoration techniques.

Building a robust business model canvas is a crucial step to start your restoration and resale business. It captures the essence of your enterprise, assisting you to create, deliver and capture value. It's the comprehensive guide that can lead you from a passionate hobbyist to an unstoppable entrepreneur in the furniture restoration and resale industry. Stay tuned to this guide, as it delves deeper into each of these aspects, providing you with the inspiration, practical advice, and unmatched commercial savvy you need to catapult your journey to success.

Chapter 7. Green Money: Incorporating Sustainability into Your Business Strategy

In a world where caring for the environment is atop priority, developing a sustainable furniture restoration business won't just be cognizant of the Earth - it could also be profitable. This journey requires a conscious and transformative approach, ensuring every aspect of the trade breathes sustainability. Let's dive into the fine details.

7.1. Assessing the Environmental Impact

Knowing is half the battle won. A key to building a green business strategy is to understand the environmental impact of your current operations. Identify all the ways your business may be affecting the environment: the raw materials, energy usage, waste production and disposal, product packaging, delivery, etc. Then look for green alternatives for each.

Consider drafting a checklist:

- Raw Material: Is the source sustainable? Is it possible to replace it with recycled or reclaimed materials?

- Energy Consumption: How much power does the restoration process require? Can you switch to renewable sources like solar or wind energy?

- Waste Management: What waste is produced during restoration? How is it managed? Think composting, recycling, and repurposing.

- Packaging: Can you switch to eco-friendly options for packaging and labeling?

- Transportation: Can you reduce carbon emissions by streamlining the delivery process?

7.2. Adopting Eco-Friendly Solutions

Once you've identified the areas of possible environmental impact, it's time to implement sustainable practices.

- Raw Materials: Instead of purchasing new furniture to restore, why not source old, discarded furniture? Various online platforms, auction houses, and yard sales could be treasure troves of raw material.

- Energy: Consider adopting renewable energy to power your operations. If installing solar panels or wind turbines is financially challenging, consider switching to an energy provider who offers renewable energy.

- Waste: Minimize the waste produced during restoration. It may take creativity: sawdust can be used as compost, leftover paint can be donated, and offcuts could serve as artistic pieces.

- Packaging: Opt for packaging made from recycled or bio-degradable materials. Your customers will appreciate the environmentally conscious approach.

- Transportation: Use energy-efficient vehicles for delivery, or partner with green shipping companies that counterbalance their carbon emissions.

7.3. Forming Green Partnerships

Form partnerships with other businesses that prioritize sustainability. This can include suppliers of eco-friendly materials, green energy providers, and recycling companies. Such associations can not only reduce your environmental footprint but also enhance your business image. Look for certifications such as FSC (Forest Stewardship Council) for wood suppliers, Green Seal for paint suppliers, etc.

7.4. Marketing Your Green Initiative

After adapting your operations to become more sustainable, it's essential to communicate these changes to your client base. People like to know they are supporting an environmentally conscious business. Hence, green marketing can be an outstanding strategy.

Create a detailed sustainability report of your business and share it on your website or social media platforms. This transparency will help you gain the trust of your customers and could attract a wider audience interested in green businesses.

Get your sustainable practices certified by recognized environmental or sustainability organizations. Such certifications can not only enhance your credibility but can also provide access to a network of green businesses and customers.

Incorporating green elements into your marketing will showcase your commitment. For instance, use green color in your promotional materials, your logo, or even adopt a slogan related to your sustainability mission.

Remember, every small step toward sustainability contributes to a larger journey. Never underestimate the potential impact of your actions.

7.5. Enhancing Financial Sustainability

While it's essential to have environmental sustainability, your business also needs to be financially sustainable. Optimize your supply chain and operations to reduce costs. Find innovative ways to upcycle the materials you have in hand, reducing the need for new purchases.

Cut down energy costs by adopting energy-efficient tools and measures. Reinvest your savings into business growth and development. Equal importance must be given to both the environment and finance to successfully run a furniture restoration business.

7.6. Continuous Improvement & Innovation

Sustainability is an ongoing journey, not a destination. It requires constant evaluation of your practices and seeking improvement opportunities. Aim for newer and better ways of integrating sustainable practices into your business - be it materials, techniques, or technologies. Ultimately, the 'green' in your green money represents more than just profit - it's a commitment to a sustainable future that puts equal emphasis on your bottom line and the environment.

In conclusion, running a furniture restoration and resale business with sustainability at its core is a challenging yet immensely rewarding journey. Follow these clear steps, and you're well on your way to creating a business that prides itself on making a significant environmental impact while simultaneously making profits. It's feasible, and it's the future.

Chapter 8. Building Your Brand: Crafting a Unique Identity in the Marketplace

In an oversaturated market, your brand is your beacon. It's what distinguishes you from the competition and beckons those who resonate with your ethos. It's not merely a logo or a catchy name; indeed, it's a full-fledged representation of who you are, what you do, and importantly, what you stand for.

8.1. Understanding Your Target Market

To succeed, you'll need to deeply understand who you're targeting. People who seek refurbished and upcycled furniture are typically those who value sustainability, appreciate creativity and respect character and history within their living spaces.

Consider the following questions as you assess your target audience: What age bracket do they fall under? What's their income range? What draws them to vintage and recycled furniture? Take ample time to research and create realistic personas that personify your typical clientele. Your brand must speak their language, understand their needs, and mirror their values.

8.2. Defining Your Unique Selling Proposition

Once you know your audience, you should focus on defining your unique selling proposition (USP). What about your products or services can't be found elsewhere? It could be your focus on exclusively recycling specific types of furniture, your clever reinvention techniques, or the exceptional durability of your finishes.

A unique identifier strengthens your brand, the same way the smell of varnish and fresh paint evokes the atmosphere of a craftsman's workshop. It's this distinction that will make your company memorable, helping to earn your customers' loyalty and support.

8.3. Crafting Your Brand Design

Arguably one most identifiable aspects of your brand is your visual design. This encompasses your logo, color palette, typography, imagery and overall aesthetic. It should reflect your company's personality as well as your unique selling proposition.

For instance, if your refurbished furniture maintains its antique aesthetic, a vintage-inspired design may resonate well with your audience. Alternatively, if your furniture receives a modern twist, a brand design that's sleek, minimalist or edgy may be more suitable.

8.4. Establishing Your Brand Voice

Your brand voice is the tone in which you communicate with your audience. This includes content on your website, social media posts, product descriptions, and customer service interactions.

For instance, if your upcycled furniture brings joy and humor to the home (say, a table made from a surfboard), your brand voice might be playful and light-hearted. If your products are about luxury and opulence, your brand voice could be more formal and refined.

8.5. Building a Captivating Brand Story

Brand storytelling is a powerful tool that can imbue your business with depth and personality. This could start by narrating the journey behind launching your furniture restoration business or sharing tales of hunting for items to be restored. A compelling story can create an emotional connection with your customers, setting you apart in the market.

8.6. Homing in on Your Core Values

Your core values are the principles that guide your business. They could include your commitment to sustainability through restoring and upcycling, a dedication to quality workmanship, or a guarantee of unique, one-of-a-kind pieces. Communicating your values shows your target audience what you stand for—an important consideration for conscious shoppers choosing between similar products.

8.7. Leveraging Social Media for Brand Visibility

Once your brand is firmly established, it's time to get it seen. Begin by creating profiles on major social platforms such as Instagram, Facebook, Pinterest, and Twitter. Make sure to regularly share high-quality images of your products, behind-the-scenes process, and prompts related to vintage furniture. The key here is to consistently communicate your brand's voice and aesthetic while engaging with your audience.

Build a brand that stands the test of time. This isn't a one-time event but rather, a continuous process that should move and evolve with your business and its audience. Craft your identity with care, infuse it with your passion for furniture restoration and let it be a reflection of your craftsmanship, making sure it stands out in a crowd. Your brand is your legacy, so build it to last.

Chapter 9. How to Price it Right: Understanding Costing and Pricing for Profit

Establishing your pricing strategy when refurbishing and reselling furniture forms the bedrock for a profitable business model. The numbers behind the facelift for an old chair or vintage desk must carefully be worked out and successfully translated into a price your customers are inclined to pay. However, this crucial first step doesn't happen devoid of insight and planning. It requires a deep understanding of cost components, market dynamics, demographic preferences, and more.

9.1. The Fundamental Components of Costs

Every furniture restoration project entails a unique blend of costs, determined by the complexity of the restoration, the original price, and the materials used. When setting a price, start by examining the fundamental components of costs:

Cost of Acquisition: This is the upfront purchase price you pay to acquire the furniture. In some cases, however, the initial outlay might be insignificant or even zero if, for example, the furniture has been given to you or found abandoned.

Materials: Every project will require a range of different restoration materials like paint, varnish, wood fillers, upholstery fabrics, foams, screws, or even replacement parts. The cost of such materials must be factored in.

Labor: Whether you're restoring furniture by yourself, employing manpower, or outsourcing skilled work such as upholstery, it's important to factor the cost of labor. Time spent is money expended.

Overheads: These include indirect costs, like rent for your workspace, bills for electricity, and tools maintenance. They might also encompass marketing and advertising expenses.

9.2. Step-by-Step Calculation of Costs

Once the cost components are identified, the next step is to calculate the total cost of each item you propose to sell. Take every single expense into account — from the initial purchase through restoration to the final marketing. For example:

- Item acquisition: $50
- Materials (paint, upholstery fabrics, screws): $70
- Labor (10 hours x $20/hr): $200
- Overhead (estimated for this item): $30
- Total: $350

This is the final cost of the item, i.e., the amount of money that will go from your pocket for this piece to be fully restored—with your time bill also included and overhead averaged over the number of pieces you work on.

9.3. Markup and Profit Margin

Determining the markup is key to setting your final selling price. Markup is a percentage of the cost price that covers overhead and generates a profit. An industry standard to start from is a 50% markup, but you could opt for a premium when dealing with high-end or distinctive pieces that may fetch a higher price due to exclusivity or exceptional craftsmanship.

Taking the previous figure of $350, if we apply a 50% markup:

- Cost: $350

- Markup (50% of $350): $175

- Selling Price: $525

Note that the markup percentage may vary based on various factors such as uniqueness, degree of restoration, and artistic value.

9.4. Understand Market Prices

Mapping your prices with the current market rates is crucial. Spend time regularly to study market prices and trends and get a feel for a suitable selling price. Online marketplaces, antique stores, and auctions can provide benchmarks. Understanding the price range will prevent you from underselling or overshooting customer expectations.

9.5. Pricing for Specific Demographics

If you are targeting a specific demographic, like high-end customers or budget-conscious customers, your costs, markup, and selling price need alignment with their expectations. Custom or bespoke furniture restoration often warrants higher fees, and customers usually are ready to bear these costs for personalized experiences.

9.6. Building Value to Justify Price

A practical and aesthetic piece of furniture has inherent value. However, its value further escalates with the narrative—the charm of the old, the careful hours spent restoring it, its environmental friendliness—an important USP, especially for environment-conscious buyers.

By emphasizing these factors, you build a compelling story that can justify a higher price for your furniture. The beauty of the narrative is that it can pull customers towards your brand, building the authenticity and trust that transforms transactions into relationships.

9.7. Adjusting Pricing Based on Demand

Prices should never be static. Stay flexible and ready to adjust your prices based on demand, competition, changes in costs of materials, and global economic factors. It can fluctuate to some extent, keeping the local market dynamics in mind.

Pricing refurbished furniture is both an art and a science. Start with a clear understanding and calculation of costs, add a well-reasoned markup, and simulate market prices. Always consider your target demographic and tweak the price to increase the perceived value of your products. This dynamic and calculated approach to pricing will set the foundation for a successful and long-lasting furniture restoration and resale business.

Chapter 10. Digital Avenue: Establishing Your Online Presence & E-commerce Store

Establishing your online presence and launching an e-commerce store are vital steps in a furniture restoration and resale business. In the digital age, your online identity becomes the face of your brand, reaching customers you may never meet physically, while your e-commerce store turns into an open market for your refurbished goods - open around the clock.

10.1. Building a Strong Online Presence

Before you dive into building your e-commerce store, focus on creating a robust online presence. This presence represents who you are as a brand, drawing potential clients to your store.

Your online presence spans several digital landscapes such as your website, social media, online directories, and review sites. Start out by building a professional website – your digital storefront. Ensure it reflects your brand effectively and is easy to navigate.

Your website should efficiently communicate what you offer – professional photographs of your unique furniture pieces coupled with compelling descriptions. Make sure the information about your business – like the address, contact details, and hours of operations – is accurate and easy to find. Also, integrate your blog into your website if you plan on having one.

Next, claim your listings in online directories and review sites. This step improves your visibility and search engine ranking. Encourage satisfied customers to leave reviews and respond promptly and diplomatically to any negative feedback.

Social media platforms are crucial to spreading your branding message. Make sure to regularly share engaging content, interact with your audience, and leverage these platforms for customer service.

10.2. Setting up Your E-commerce Store

When it comes to setting up your e-commerce store, there are several factors you need to consider to ensure success and profitability.

Choose a reliable e-commerce platform that suits your business needs. Research various platforms like Shopify, WooCommerce, or Magento to see which one aligns with your needs in terms of functionality, ease of use, pricing, and support.

Your e-commerce store should feel intuitive and user-friendly. Organize your products logically and use high-quality, professional photographs. Write clear, compelling product descriptions and make the checkout process simple and seamless.

10.3. SEO and Optimizing your Website

Search engine optimization (SEO) is a vital part of your online strategy. SEO affects how your website appears in search engine results, which impacts your visibility and the amount of traffic your site attracts.

For your content to perform well, it needs to be easy to read and relevant to your audience. Include keywords that potential customers might use when searching for your products but avoid keyword stuffing as it might lead to penalties.

You should also look at on-page SEO, ensuring that title tags, meta descriptions, and URLs are all optimized for your keyword. Create a sitemap to help search engines understand your website structure.

10.4. Promoting Your Store and Products Online

Promotions and marketing are key to attracting customers to your e-commerce store. Social media platforms like Instagram and Pinterest can be instrumental in showcasing your furniture, with visually appealing pictures and posts related to your products.

Email marketing is an effective method for promoting your products, discounts, and special events. Building an email list allows you to reach out to interested customers directly.

Online advertising (like Google Ads and Facebook Advertising) can help promote your store to a broader audience. You can target specific demographics, locations and interests to attract your ideal customers.

Remember to track your promotional efforts with tools like Google Analytics to determine what's working and what needs improvement.

Following these steps will help create a strong online presence and build an efficient e-commerce store. As you embark on this journey, remember it's not just about selling furniture; it's about sharing your passion for restored vintage beauty and making connections with customers who share that passion. As you meet success, stay committed to learning and evolving. After all, the digital landscape is ever-evolving around user behaviors and technological advancements. Continuity, consistency, and regular updating will keep your online business flourishing.

Overall, a furniture restoration and resale business is a viable green business model. Not only does it offer an opportunity to reduce waste and promote sustainable consumption, but it also provides an avenue for you to turn your passion into profit. By establishing a robust online presence and a seamless e-commerce store, you can reach a broader audience, increase sales, and contribute positively to the environment.

Embrace the digital avenue, breathe new life into old furniture, and let the world witness the charm of restored vintage beauty!

Chapter 11. Marketing Magic: Winning Strategies for Your Furniture Business

Marketing, by its very nature, is fluid, constantly evolving with time. Effective marketing strategies should reflect dynamism too, incorporating new trends while leaning on historically successful methods. Let's embark on a journey through the tried, tested and innovative techniques which could transform your furniture restoration and resale business's fortunes.

11.1. Crafting Your Unique Selling Proposition (USP)

Understanding what makes your business unique is the cornerstone of your marketing strategy. No two restoration businesses are alike, and yours shouldn't be the exception. Your USP is the specific, unique benefit that distinguishes your business from others.

Identify qualities, whether in your processes, your skillsets, or your products. Do you specialize in restoring a certain type of furniture? Do you offer unmatched turn-around times? Or perhaps you utilize environmentally friendly refurbishing methods? Whatever it is, encapsulate it in a short, compelling statement, your USP – the heart of all your marketing messages.

11.2. Mastering Local SEO

Local SEO refers to the process of optimizing your online presence to attract more business from local searches on Google. For furniture restoration and resale businesses, local customers are key. Begin by utilizing Google My Business to create a listing for your business. Ensure you fill out every piece of information including location, opening hours, and contact details.

Your website content should be SEO-friendly, featuring location-specific keywords and phrases to attract local searches. Google reviews can significantly influence your ranking in search results, so encourage satisfied customers to post reviews.

11.3. Harnessing Social Media

Social media platforms like Instagram and Pinterest are visual by nature, making them ideal for showcasing your restored furniture pieces. To take full advantage, develop a consistent posting schedule, use high-quality images, and engage with your followers through comments and direct messages.

On Facebook, utilize the Marketplace to sell items and join local community groups centered around furniture and home decor. There's no one-size-fits-all social media strategy, so monitor your analytics to understand what content resonates most with your audience, then adjust accordingly.

11.4. Leveraging Content Marketing

A content-rich website can help position your business as an industry expert, build deeper relationships with clients, and enhance SEO. Develop a blog with restoration tips, before-and-after pictures, or articles showcasing the history of certain furniture styles. Videos demonstrating your restoration process can also generate interest and trust.

11.5. Running Targeted Ad Campaigns

Run paid ad campaigns on social media platforms or Google targeting users within your geographic area. To get better ROI, segment your audience based on their interests, demographics or purchasing behavior. Pair these campaigns with enticing offers like discounts on their first purchase or free delivery.

11.6. Establishing Partnerships

Partner with local businesses, interior designers, or real estate agents. Mutual referrals can introduce a steady stream of customers to your business. Additionally, consider partnering with local artists or artisans to offer exclusive, upgraded pieces.

11.7. Offering Exceptional Customer Service

Superlative customer service turns one-time buyers into repeat customers and advocates for your brand. Provide educational resources, answer questions promptly and thoughtfully, and always go the extra mile to exceed expectations.

11.8. Hosting Workshops and Events

Hosting community events or workshops not only spreads the word about your business but also helps build a local base of loyal customers. These could be restoration workshops, furniture painting classes, or even regular community flea markets.

11.9. Implementing a Referral Program

Word-of-mouth marketing can be your strongest ally. Develop a referral program that offers incentives for every new customer referred – whether discounts, services, or small freebies, every gesture counts.

Remember, successful marketing is about telling your business's unique story. Add authenticity, consistency, and passion to your marketing mix, and watch as your restoration enterprise flourishes like never before.